# Prayers from the Cross

## Solace for All Seasons

*by*
John P. Mossi, S.J.

*Illustrated by*
Gertrud Mueller Nelson

PAULIST PRESS
New York/Mahwah, N.J.

imprimi potest
John A. Privett, S.J.
Provincial
California Province of the Society of Jesus
February 25, 1994

Library of Congress Cataloging-in-Publication Data

Mossi, John P.
    Prayers from the cross  :  solace for all seasons / by John P. Mossi; illus-trated by Gertrud Mueller Nelson.
        p.    cm.
    Includes bibliographical references.
    ISBN 0-8091-3524-8  (pbk.)
    1. Jesus Christ—Seven last words—Meditations.    I. Title.
BT456.M67    1994                                            94-34750
232.96'35—dc20                                               CIP

Published by Paulist Press
997 Macarthur Boulevard
Mahwah, New Jersey 07430

Printed and bound in the
United States of America

# CONTENTS

# INTRODUCTION

The lyrics of the African-American spiritual "Were You There When They Crucified My Lord?" evoke both the scene and the mood of Good Friday. Its melody causes us to ponder, to tremble interiorly, and to meditate on the redemptive event that occurred on Calvary. On that special Friday, which is described as "Good," Jesus was crucified for us so that the reconciliation of all humanity would be accomplished.

The Passion Accounts are the oldest sections of the Christian Scriptures. Hence, they hold an important memory of the early church and are a valuable touchstone of the teachings of Jesus. As contemporary disciples, these accounts help us to grapple with our own dark night experiences. Jesus assists us to address our own forms of suffering, abandonment and crucifixion. Through these bitter moments, Jesus shows us how to forgive, how to love, how to embrace life in the midst of trial and death.

While the other sections of the gospel record the miracles, parables, and activities of the ministry of Jesus, the Passion can be approached as Jesus' final opportunity to communicate the essence of his life and spirit. Jesus, even in his dying moments, reveals to us how to live as disciples and how to pray as Christians.

It is critical to remember that these costly words of Jesus were spoken for our sake. The spirituality of the Seven Last

Words is a unique, precious treasure for us to embrace and to imitate. Archbishop Oscar Romero, the six Jesuits along with the housekeeper and her fifteen year old daughter, all assassinated in El Salvador, witness to the reality of the Passion which still continues in our modern day world.

Good Friday is in many ways the last temptation of Jesus. Jesus tempts us to be totally human and vulnerable and to surrender all to God. Jesus asks us, even in the confusion of darkness and the angst of dying, to pray.

The following meditations were developed from a series of Good Friday sermons first given at Our Lady of Sorrows Catholic Community in Santa Barbara, and most recently at St. Ignatius Church in San Francisco. My goal in designing these reflections was to engage the entire assembly so that they could apply the Last Words to daily life.

*Prayers from the Cross* follows a similar intent. The book's purpose is threefold: first, to provide the necessary Passion texts so that the power of scripture may speak directly to our experience; second, to offer reflections on each saying of Jesus in order to unfold its wisdom; third, to present questions so that the reader can adapt the gospel to everyday experience.

Each chapter is divided into five sections: Theme, Scripture, Reflection, Suggestions for Action, and Prayer. The goal of each chapter is quite simple: to uncover the mature spirituality and solace of the Passion as a resource when we face our trials. In this sense, *Prayers from the Cross* is a book that is not just appropriate for the liturgical season of Lent, but really its wisdom applies throughout the entire year, whenever we encounter the cross.

The Seven Last Words are collectively found in Matthew, Luke, Mark, and John. No one gospel contains all seven. They have been organized through a traditional preaching devotion referred to in Latin as *Tre Ore*, signifying the Three Hours Jesus hung on the cross. Here is the scriptural arrangement, with an added epilogue text, chosen for this book:

1) "Father, forgive them, they know not what they do." *Luke 23:34.*

2) "Amen, I say to you, today you will be with me in Paradise." *Luke 23:43.*

3) "Woman, behold, your son."... "Behold, your mother." *John 19:26-27.*

4) "My God, my God, why have you forsaken me?" *Matthew 27:46, Mark 15:34.*

5) "I thirst." *John 19:28.*

6) "Father, into your hands I commend my spirit." *Luke 23:46.*

7) "It is finished." *John 19:30.*

8) "Jesus himself drew near and walked with them." *Luke 24:15.*

The gospels of Luke and John record the death of Jesus with different final sayings. Traditionally, the Seven Last Words have ended with Luke 23:46. I have chosen to conclude with John 19:30 as the seventh word. My reason for this adaptation is to create an interlocking prayer structure from the fourth through seventh words.

Finally, in order to connect the Passion with the resurrection, this book closes with an Epilogue that culminates in the rising of Jesus from the dead on Easter. In this way, the events of Calvary can be appreciated and clarified by the light of the resurrection.

# THE FIRST WORD

# *Forgiveness*

*"Father, forgive them,
they know not what they do." Luke 23:34*

We situate this first prayer of Jesus within the textual environment of Luke. This will be the way in which we shall ponder the Seven Last Words, always with a respect for the larger scripture mosaic in which these words are found.

## SCRIPTURE

*Again Pilate addressed them, still wishing to release Jesus, but they continued their shouting, "Crucify him! Crucify him!" Pilate addressed them a third time, "What evil has this man done? I found him guilty of no capital crime. Therefore I shall have him flogged and then release him." With loud shouts, however, they persisted in calling for his crucifixion, and their voices prevailed. The verdict of Pilate was that their demand should be granted. So he released the man who had been imprisoned for rebellion and murder, for whom they asked, and he handed Jesus over to them to deal with as they wished.*

*As they led him away they took hold of a certain Simon, a Cyrenian, who was coming in from the country; and after laying the cross on him, they made him carry it behind Jesus. A large crowd of people followed Jesus, including many women who mourned and lamented him. Jesus turned to them and said, "Daughters of Jerusalem, do not weep for me; weep instead for yourselves and for your children, for indeed, the days are coming when people will say, 'Blessed are the barren, the wombs that never bore and the breasts that never nursed.' At that time people will say to the mountains, 'Fall on us!' and to the hills, 'Cover us!' for if these things are done when the wood is green what will happen when it is dry?" Now two others, both criminals, were led away with him to be executed.*

*When they came to the place called the Skull, they crucified* him and the criminals there, one on his right, the other on his left. Then Jesus said, "Father, forgive them, they know not what they do." Luke 23:20-34.

## REFLECTION

Let us revisit some of the realities of this Calvary scene. Jesus now hangs as a condemned criminal on the cross. He is naked, alone, in extreme pain. The crown of thorns torments his head. Blood runs over his eyes. Rough iron nails pierce his hands and feet. The interior of Jesus is a sea of sorrow and anguish.

At the foot of the cross stand the skeptics and guards who listen for what Jesus might say. Some indifferently watch, others mock and jeer. The leaders taunt, "He saved others, let him save himself if he is the chosen one, the Messiah of God." Luke 23:35. Some, no doubt, felt a divine favor has been done by eliminating a false prophet. The soldiers, after offering Jesus vinegar to drink, add their own scorn, "If you are King of the Jews, save yourself." Luke 23:37.

Questions assault our mind. We ask, "Is this the victory of darkness?" "What has Jesus done to merit such hostility, cruelty, and malice?" When we ourselves, or those dear to us, or the innocent, experience similar injustice and pain, we angrily question, "Why does God let this happen?"

What would have been our own first word if we were crushed under the weight of such despair? If we had the ability and the power, how would we have settled the score? Perhaps clenched our fists in anger and exterminated those at our feet?

And Jesus? His response? He prays. He allies himself with life. He prays to the Father. He prays forgiveness. He invokes pardon. He prays from the heart.

Jesus does not deny the evil, the darkness, the injustice. He transforms it with compassion. In effect, Jesus models for us a spirituality of forgiveness. First, focus on the Father who is the source of true forgiveness. Second, pray in conjunction with the Father to forgive all enemies. Third, pray for the divine insight that the aggression of evil is the result of not knowing the love of God. In the prayer of the first word, Jesus calls upon the tender mercy of the Father to pardon and forgive those who seek his death.

During the Penitential Rite of Mass, we pray a litany for growth in this necessary quality of mercy:

> Lord, have mercy.
> Christ, have mercy.
> Lord, have mercy.

We petition to be living sacraments of God's mercy to others, aware that the Father is always compassionate toward us every second of every day, no matter how poorly we respond. If God would ever fail to be so unconditionally compassionate and full of loving mercy toward us, even for a few moments, we and all creation would cease to exist. St. Paul, addressing the citizens of Athens in Acts 17:28, reflects on the totality of God's pervasive, continuous love for each one of us, "In him we live and move and have our being." God, the most merciful and compassionate one, cannot deny his very nature.

From the cross, Jesus invites us for the last time to love our enemies, to recommend them to the Father, to pray for them. To respond to the reality of darkness, not with darkness, but with the light of forgiveness and love.

However, we cannot omit Jesus' phrase, "They know not what they do." What is your reaction to these words? Does not Jesus pardon his persecutors lightly with an implausible excuse? Exactly, what does this mean, "They know not what they do"? Is it tantamount to saying that Judas did not know his act of betrayal when he kissed Jesus? The crowd did not know they were shouting, "Crucify him! Crucify him!"? Are we exempt from the knowledge and consequences of what we do? When we sin, do we do so through ignorance? When someone robs a grocery store, shoots the manager, and runs over an innocent bystander, is this person without culpability?

Since childhood, we know right from wrong. We know when we choose light and when we choose darkness. Is Jesus making a weak excuse for our inhumanity? Or is he saying something more profound? That is, there is one great reality that we don't know when we sin and choose evil: what we don't know is the overwhelming love of God for us.

In sin, we become trapped in our own addictiveness and gratification. In sin, we block the love of God. In sin, we postpone the knowledge and the love of God from living in us, and through us touching others. Jesus was in constant contact with this higher mercy and love of the Father. Hence, he could truly understand and pray, "Father, forgive them, they know not what they do."

## SUGGESTIONS FOR ACTION

The living gospel continually invites us to make this first prayer of Jesus our own. To be a disciple means to pray as Jesus gives us example, "Father, forgive them."

We do so in four important steps. Apply the necessary time that each step requires.

First, call to mind anyone who has hurt you, insulted you, or committed the offense which is impossible to erase from memory. This individual or group may be living or dead, a member of the family, a neighbor, a friend, a teacher, a priest or religious, a co-worker, someone who belongs to your club or association. Bring this person to mind.

Next, as you see this person you despise, ask Jesus for the gift to forgive and to love that person as he does.

Third, center your attention completely on Jesus. Focus on his loving courage and the way he teaches us how to forgive.

Look directly into the eyes of Jesus until you can join with him in saying to those who hurt you, "Father, forgive them."

Fourth, as you continue to pray for forgiveness, place this person in the healing love of Jesus. Hand over the memories of the painful experience to Jesus in whose hands such memories belong. Finally, pray from the heart, asking the Father to bless that person.

Such a prayer of forgiveness is seldom easy to achieve the first time. To forgive one's enemies demands the purest love. Often we have to repeat the process again and again. When forgiveness is especially problematic to attain, do not attempt to pray alone. Call on the assistance of the Holy Spirit. It is important to keep fixed on the unconditional way that Jesus instructs us to forgive.

## PRAYER

Recite slowly the Our Father. Give special attention to its petitions for forgiveness.

# THE SECOND WORD

## *To Give Away Heaven*

*"Amen, I say to you,
today you will be with me in Paradise." Luke 23:43*

Let us once again enhance our meditation with a more complete text of the Word of God.


**SCRIPTURE**
*Now one of the criminals hanging there reviled Jesus, saying, "Are you not the Messiah? Save yourself and us." The other, however, rebuking him, said in reply, "Have you no fear of God, for you are subject to the same condemnation? And indeed, we have been condemned justly, for the sentence we received corresponds to our crimes, but this man has done nothing criminal." Then he said, "Jesus, remember me when you come into your kingdom." He replied to him, "Amen, I say to you, today you will be with me in Paradise." Luke 23:39-43.*


**REFLECTION**
There is a classic legend that when Mary and Joseph fled into Egypt with the child Jesus, they rested at a roadside inn. Mary asked the hostess for water to bathe Jesus. The hostess then requested if she could bathe her own child, who was suffering from leprosy, in the same water in which Jesus was immersed. The sick infant, upon touching the water, was instantly healed of the disease.

The legend continues that this cured child grew in strength and became a clever thief. He is the criminal, traditionally referred to as Dismas and called the Good Thief, who hangs on his own cross to the right of Jesus.

Let us consider the Good Thief, and then, Jesus. What do they each have to teach about prayer and heaven? The lesson is uncomplicated: it is never too late. St. Paul reminds us in 2

Corinthians 6:2, "Behold, now is a very acceptable time; behold, now is the day of salvation."

As we hover over this Calvary scene, Jesus receives little sympathy or consolation. The people jeer, "Save yourself." The chief priests and scribes mock, "Come down from the cross that we may see and believe." The soldiers taunted as well and offered vinegar. The other thief joined in the abuse, "Save yourself and, of course, don't forget to include us too."

The only one to speak to Jesus with any compassion, with any note of concern, is the thief on the right. He acknowledges that he is receiving what he deserves. The Good Thief speaks for us all. "We deserve the cross, not the Innocent One. We receive the consequences of what we have merited, but what action has Jesus done to merit crucifixion and to die as a criminal?"

In dramatic contrast to all those present, the Good Thief addresses Jesus by name and in supplication. Dismas teaches us how to pray at the last minute, in the midst of difficulty, even in the face of death. The thief, ready for conversion, calls out in friendship to Jesus. Dismas is the only one on Calvary to speak to Jesus by name. He creates an inspiring, brief prayer: "Jesus, remember me when you come into your kingdom." Dismas, during his quickly disappearing time on earth, expresses the desire to be associated with Jesus and his kingdom.

These final words of the thief are a gentle supplication, a last petition and, perhaps, his very first plea as well. In Luke 11:9, Jesus invites us to ask, to seek, to knock. "And I tell you, ask and you will receive; seek and you will find; knock and the door will be opened to you." Maybe the thief appealed this one time only, sought this one time only, knocked this one time only. He risked everything and in return found the pearl of great price. The Good Thief provides us with needed courage which affirms that it is never too late to reach out to Jesus. It is never too late to seek reconciliation with our Savior. That day, Jesus entered heaven with an exceptionally "good thief." In a real sense, Dismas died a thief, having stolen heaven.

There is a refreshing story about Jesus appearing to a devout woman. She mentioned this favored encounter to her bishop who doubted the authenticity of this experience. He decided to test her story with a query. "When Jesus appears to you the next time, ask him to mention the specific sins of your bishop." A month later the devout woman returned and mentioned that she again had conversation with Jesus. "Did you ask Jesus my question?" "Yes, bishop, I did." "And what did he say?" Jesus said, "He doesn't remember your sins anymore."

In the first word, Jesus models for us how to forgive. In this second word, Jesus forgets instantaneously our track record in order to open the gates of heaven. The exchange between Jesus and the Good Thief is a reminder that Jesus is ever anxious to extend heaven to us no matter what we have done. Even at our last breath, it is never too late to pray with the Good Thief: "Jesus, remember me when you come into your kingdom."

The reassuring words of Luke 23:43 are for anyone who desires to be a follower of Jesus, "This day you shall be with me in Paradise." The overwhelming reality and insight of the second word is that Jesus is solicitous to give away heaven. He places no conditions whenever we turn to him. In fact, it is impossible for Jesus not to lavish us with heaven.

## SUGGESTIONS FOR ACTION

As we reflect on this second word of Jesus, we can ask ourselves how we can give away heaven as well. The Seven Last Words of Jesus are like summary instructions, training manuals for his followers. They challenge us to be more Christ-like.

Heaven is dispensed in diverse ways. To give away our love, compassion, time, talents and skills are some different ways of making the kingdom of God genuine. To give away that heavenly gift that will lighten another person's cross makes paradise apparent today.

It is important to give heaven away not just to close friends but to the faceless, the homeless, the nameless, those whom society considers as outcast and non-important, those who are most in need of respect and dignity. In our petitions asking Jesus to remember us in our need, our response should always be to remember others, especially the marginal, in their plight.

1) Ask Jesus to show you those unique aspects of heaven you can give away. Your gift might be in the form of volunteer work, the donated help of a specific skill or knowledge, certain talents, or financial assistance. Spend time in conversation with Jesus considering how you can best imitate his generosity on the cross.

2) Next, ask Jesus to present to you the faces of those in need of what you can give. Mother Teresa reminds us that we do not have to travel to distant lands to find and serve the poor. Often the needy are in our own neighborhood and cities, not to mention in our families and social groups.

3) Finally, as you ponder the crucified one, ask Jesus for the courage, gospel imagination and strength to take the first important step: to make that phone call, to establish that contact, to offer your services, to make a donation. The second step is similar: to develop the attitude to give away heaven spontaneously as an habitual way of life.

## PRAYER
Teach me, Jesus,
to serve you as you deserve;
   to give and not to count the cost;

to fight and not to heed the wounds;
   to toil and not to seek for rest;
to labor and not to ask for any reward,
   save that of knowing
that I do your will.

*St. Ignatius of Loyola*

# THE THIRD WORD

# *Community*

*"Woman, behold, your son."*
*"Behold, your mother." John 19:26-27*

Again, let us contextualize this third word with its surrounding verses.

## SCRIPTURE
*When the soldiers had crucified Jesus, they took his clothes and divided them into four shares, a share for each soldier. They also took his tunic, but the tunic was seamless, woven in one piece from the top down. So they said to one another, "Let's not tear it, but cast lots for it to see whose it will be," in order that the passage of scripture might be fulfilled [that says]:*

"They divided my garments among them,
and for my vesture they cast lots."

*This is what the soldiers did. Standing by the cross of Jesus were his mother and his mother's sister, Mary the wife of Clopas, and Mary of Magdala. When Jesus saw his mother and the disciple there whom he loved, he said to his mother, "Woman, behold, your son." Then he said to the disciple, "Behold, your mother." And from that hour the disciple took her into his home. John 19:23-27.*

## REFLECTION
It is not surprising that at the foot of the cross we find Mary, the first believer and foremost disciple, the mother of Jesus. Mary is surrounded by a small community of believers: Mary Clopas, Mary Magdalene, and the beloved disciple. Matthew 27:56 also includes Salome, the mother of the sons of

Zebedee. It is interesting to note that the women on Calvary outnumber the men four to one.

There is mentioned "the disciple whom he loved." Tradition tells us this is the Apostle John. However, scripture does not name the beloved disciple as John. This disciple is anonymous. In many ways, this disciple is every unnamed believer. Each one of us as a believer, as a person of faith, can insert our own name in the company of this group of disciples. For what disciple is there, no matter how weak, that Jesus does not consider as beloved?

Let us consider two special ways in which Mary is present on Calvary: first, as a disciple; second, as a person of faith.

Mary is the first disciple of Jesus. No one heard the Word of God better and responded to the Word more fully than Mary. She opened herself so completely to the Holy Spirit that through her the Word became flesh. St. Augustine in the fourth century speaks of Mary in this way: "She first conceived Jesus in her heart before conceiving him in her womb." It is in this role as the first and foremost disciple of Jesus that Mary is present on Calvary. Her following of Jesus is so total, so encompassing, even when this means standing at the foot of the cross, that it is literally inconceivable for Mary not to be there.

Mary is also present as a person of faith. As a young person, she humbly said "yes" to the invitation by the Holy Spirit to be the Mother of God. She literally surrendered her person and journey to the providential care of God. Like us, she had no idea of the future turns in her faith journey, those surprises and the setbacks that are the consequences of being a follower of Christ. As a person of faith, she put her whole life at stake acknowledging that God is present and active, not only in the joyful events of the Christian pilgrimage, but on Calvary as well.

To be a person of faith, associated with Jesus, demands total commitment. At the foot of the cross, Mary perhaps recalled the words that Simeon addressed to her when he blessed the child Jesus at the temple in Jerusalem: "And you yourself a sword will pierce." Luke 2:35. From the beginning of her pilgrimage, Mary understood that she would intimately share in the sufferings of her son. The fulfillment of Simeon's words came when Mary held the limp body of the Crucified in her arms. She would know first-hand, and better than anyone else, the truth revealed in the Pietà.

One would think that the privilege of being the mother of Jesus would have somehow exempted Mary from Calvary. She was not dispensed, no more than Jesus was spared. Nor are we exempt. On Calvary, Jesus makes a profound statement. He enters into total solidarity with our human condition, even the ambiguous questioning that surrounds dying and the dark finality of death. Jesus, accepting the fullness of his humanity, chose to remain present on the cross. He reveals for us that the spirit of God was not absent from the mystery of Calvary. Daringly, Jesus helps us find God in the midst of suffering and darkness.

Let us try to plumb the intensity of this third prayer of Jesus. It is a selfless expression. Even to the very last, Jesus diverts attention from himself and invites those present to minister to one another. Jesus encourages us all to create community, to recognize one another, to enter into relationships. This art of building community is twofold: first, to behold others; second, to uphold and care for neighbor and stranger.

To Mary, Jesus asks that she now behold her new son. To the beloved disciple, Jesus entrusts his mother as essential to his household. The wisdom from the cross that Jesus imparts is most obvious. Our task as God's chosen people, as parishioners, as neighbors, as family, is to pass beyond the barriers of isolation, to behold one another, to enter into deeper interpersonal relationships. Membership in community for Jesus is not an option, it is a way of serving in his spirit.

Jesus in his act of dying is still creating community. He creates church, a new set of relationships where disciples are responsive to God and to one another. In Matthew 12:49-50,

Jesus describes this new family of God, in which the only consideration lies in being related to Jesus as a brother, sister, or mother and to do God's will:

> And stretching out his hand toward his disciples, he said, "Here are my mother and my brothers. For whoever does the will of my heavenly Father is my brother, and sister, and mother."

This third instruction of Jesus asks us to embrace one another in reverence. Jesus does not desire that anyone on Calvary stand alone, as estranged, or passive. The challenge of Calvary demands that we even use the cross to find and behold each another. In the demanding process of building church we are called to overcome the darkness of Calvary which can blur creative vision. The outward response of Jesus is to behold and be attentive to others, thereby always making room for another sojourner.

## SUGGESTIONS FOR ACTION

For our prayer meditation, let us learn from Mary, a mother of great faith and the first disciple of Jesus. Ask her for the grace and strength to face those personal Calvarys we shudder to endure. She stood at the cross. How can her wisdom and fortitude help us to address those realities we cannot change?

Focus upon one experience, event, relationship that is particularly difficult for you to face. Ask Mary to show the way. How was she, as a disciple, able to stand in solidarity with her son on Calvary? Is there a lesson here for us?

The next intercession we direct to Jesus. Ask him for the vision to go beyond your own suffering in order to see others in their need. In the face of opposition, how can you still create community and church, beholding the stranger as brother and sister of Jesus?

Call to mind the diverse community of people you belong to. In what specific way can you be a builder of relationships for these groups?

## PRAYER

Lord, make me an instrument of your peace:
where there is hatred, let me sow love;
　where there is injury, pardon;
where there is doubt, faith;
　where there is despair, hope;
where there is darkness, light;
　and where there is sadness, joy.

Grant that I may not so much seek to be
consoled as to console;
　to be understood, as to understand,
to be loved, as to love;
　for it is in giving that we receive,
it is in pardoning that we are pardoned,
　and it is in dying that we are born to eternal life.

*St. Francis of Assisi*

# THE FOURTH WORD

# *To Pray from the Depths*

*"My God, my God, why have you forsaken me?"*
*Matthew 27:46*

## SCRIPTURE

*From noon onward, darkness came over the whole land until three in the afternoon. And about three o'clock Jesus cried out in a loud voice, "Eli, Eli, lema sabachthani?" which means, "My God, my God, why have you forsaken me?" Some of the bystanders who heard it said, "This one is calling for Elijah." Immediately one of them ran to get a sponge; he soaked it in wine, and putting it on a reed, gave it to him to drink. But the rest said, "Wait, let us see if Elijah comes to save him."* Matthew 27.45-49.

## REFLECTION

Jesus addressed his first three prayers to three different groups. The first, to his persecutors, "Father, forgive them." The second, to sinners, "Today you will be with me in Paradise." The third, to his disciples, "Woman, behold, your son." ... "Behold, your mother."

The next two petitions, the fourth and the fifth, reveal the personal sufferings of Jesus on the cross. The fourth word illustrates the angst of one rejected by God, "My God, my God, why have you forsaken me?" The fifth word shows the interior suffering of the humanity of Jesus, "I thirst."

With each of these words, Jesus continues to demonstrate to us how to live, how to die, and how to pray.

John of the Cross, the Spanish mystic of the sixteenth century, wrote about the "Dark Night of the Senses." It is that state of being and prayer when all consolation, interior peace and strength are absent, not felt. The spiritual senses seem dead.

John of the Cross then went on to describe what he referred to as the "Dark Night of the Soul." This is when even

31

a sliver of God's presence is absent. The soul feels abandoned, rejected, orphaned. The isolation becomes crushing.
Both emotionally and spiritually, the Dark Night experience
rips apart and disintegrates any remaining, however minute,
affinity with God.

In such a total Dark Night state we encounter this fourth
prayer of Jesus. These are words of anger and rage. "My God,
my God, why have you done this to me?" We have all
expressed such sentiments at one time or another. It is that hor-
rible, wrenching time when the forces of night seem to prevail,
and the abyss separating us from God seems insurmountable.

And what does Jesus do? His response? He prays. He prays
in and through the darkness. Jesus continues to cry out to
God whom he senses as not present. Jesus prays from the
depths of his person, from his emotional core. There is no
denial, he is very much in touch with his excruciating pain. In
fact, Jesus actively uses his emptiness, anguish, and abandonment as the beginning point of prayer.

On Calvary, Jesus teaches us to pray. The prayer of this
fourth word has four parts:

1) Be in touch with the wellsprings of your depths and the
   resources of your experience. In one's emotions a direct-
   ness and intensity in prayer are found.

2) Next, call on the Creator. Let these be your first words.
   Make the prayer personal, "My God, my God."

3) Then, express the experience and the accompanying
   emotion as it is literally felt. Articulate this reality, uncen-
   sored, in its full strength. "Why have you forsaken me?"
   "I am in pain." "I don't know what to say or to believe
   anymore." "I feel lost at sea."

4) Ask Jesus for the courage to live through this time of trial, while at the same time allowing your prayer to continue to rise from your depths.

This entreaty is referred to as the prayer of the passions, a prayer most visceral and real. Jesus is comfortable praying in this manner. He gives us permission to do the same. There is no despair, raging question of why, no emotion, lamentation, or bitter agony that the Father is not able to hear.

"My God, my God, why have you forsaken me?" is the beginning verse of Psalm 22. Jesus, crying out the first line, claims the entire Psalm which ends in a confidence of vindication. Let us reflect upon some of the graphic descriptions found in this Psalm. It is the desperate cry of all the poor, powerless, and abandoned.

## PSALM 22

My God, my God, why have you abandoned me?
    Why so far from my call for help, from my cries of anguish?
My God, I call by day, but you do not answer;
    by night, but I have no relief.
Yet you are enthroned as the Holy One;
    you are the glory of Israel.
In you our ancestors trusted;
    they trusted and you rescued them.
To you they cried out and they escaped;
    in you they trusted and were not disappointed.
But I am a worm, hardly human,
    scorned by everyone, despised by the people.
All who see me mock me;
    they curl their lips and jeer;
        they shake their heads at me:
"You relied on the Lord—let him deliver you;
    if he loves you, let him rescue you."

Yet you drew me forth from the womb,
  made me safe at my mother's breast.
Upon you I was thrust from the womb;
  since birth you are my God.
Do not stay far from me,
  for trouble is near,
    and there is no one to help.

Like water my life drains away;
  all my bones grow soft.
My heart has become like wax,
  it melts away within me.
As dry as a potsherd is my throat;
  my tongue sticks to my palate;
    you lay me in the dust of death.

Many dogs surround me;
  a pack of evildoers closes in on me.
So wasted are my hands and feet
  that I can count all my bones.
They stare at me and gloat;
  they divide my garments among them;
    for my clothing they cast lots.

But you, Lord, do not stay far off;
  my strength, come quickly to help me.
Deliver me from the sword,
  my forlorn life from the teeth of the dog.
Save me from the lion's mouth,
  my poor life from the horns of wild bulls.
*Psalm 22:2-12, 15-22*

Jesus, identifying with the sentiments of these verses, admits his vulnerability and releases his lament in order to claim a deeper strength in God. Jesus demonstrates how to use our distress as a beginning point of prayer. Only through appropriating the anguish and injustice can one move through the impasse of the Dark Night.

## SUGGESTIONS FOR ACTION
In the meditation period that follows, ask Jesus for the courage to incorporate your own Dark Night experiences and emotions as important and necessary components in prayer. Reflectively consider the following three areas of examination.

1) When you are in crisis and God seems distant, how do you respond? What do your normal prayer, thought, and action pattern reveal? In what way does this fourth word of Jesus challenge and assist your spiritual growth?

2) How comfortable are you with others as they express their pain? Do you want to change the topic? Or do you attentively listen to their story and sorrow without trying to fix their feelings? The first step in healing is the handing over of the suffering to someone who is empathetic and compassionate.

3) How well do you share with others your own grief and disappointment? Do you protect yourself like a fortified city? How easily do you disclose to God in prayer your burdens and negative feelings? Who is your confidant in whom you entrust the care of your person?

## PRAYER
Take, Lord, and receive
all my liberty, my memory,
my understanding, and my entire will,
all that I have and possess.

You have given all to me.
To you, Lord, I return it.

Take, also, my sorrow,
my distress, and my darkness.
    All is yours.
Dispose of it wholly according to your will.
    Give me your love and your grace,
for this is enough for me.

*St. Ignatius of Loyola,*<br>*adapted prayer*

# THE FIFTH WORD

# *Thirsting for God*

*"I thirst." John 19:28*

## SCRIPTURE

*After this, aware that everything was now finished, in order that the scripture might be fulfilled, Jesus said, "I thirst." There was a vessel filled with common wine. So they put a sponge soaked in wine on a sprig of hyssop and put it up to his mouth. John 19:28-29.*

## REFLECTION

The parched lips of Jesus disclose his fragile humanity. Seeking momentary relief, he cries out to anyone who can hear, "I thirst." The cumulative brutality of Good Friday, beginning with the scourging at the pillar, followed by the crowning of thorns, carrying of the cross and crucifixion, reveals its toll: dehydration of body and spirit. As the blood and sweat of Jesus seep into the earth, Jesus pleads for a drink to quench his fever and pain.

Psalm 69:21-22 foreshadowed this fifth word of Jesus:

> Insult has broken my heart, and I am weak,
>> I looked for compassion, but there was none;
>> for comforters, but found none.
> Instead they put gall in my food;
>> for my thirst they gave me vinegar.

On a spiritual level, the Gospel of John points to a deeper thirst of Jesus, a thirst to complete his mission, a thirst to fulfill scripture.

Again, Jesus teaches us something about prayer. He uses his desert experience, his parched soul as a means to thirst for God. He is truly aware that his task is to fulfill scripture, to

39

finish everything the Father has given him to complete. So, even in the human experience of thirsting, Jesus is actively demonstrating to us how to live and die, not as if passively assaulted with blind fate or as a helpless victim, but intentionally, yearning for God.

John 19:34 subsequently records, "but one soldier thrust his lance into his side, and immediately blood and water flowed out." One would imagine that Jesus in his last moments would have depleted his reservoirs of strength. What possibly more could be offered? Yet, even in his dying and death, his body continues to pour out whatever remains of the sacrament of his person, namely, his redemptive blood and water.

St. Paul in the letter to the Philippians 2:6-8 praises this total donation of Jesus.

Who, though he was in the form of God,
   did not regard equality with God something to be grasped.
Rather, he emptied himself,
taking the form of a slave,
coming in human likeness;
and found human in appearance,
he humbled himself,
becoming obedient to death,
   even death on a cross.

Both the thirsting for God of Jesus and the emptying of his blood and water become images for our spiritual growth as well. As each of us experiences our own thirsting, the gospel of John invites us to partake of the two redemptive sacraments that originate in Jesus, namely, Baptism and Eucharist.

Recall the words of Jesus as he teaches us how to satiate our thirst. At the Last Supper, Jesus took the cup of blessing and said, "Drink from it, all of you, for this is my blood of the covenant, which will be shed on behalf of many for the forgiveness of sins." Matthew 26:27-28. Elsewhere, on the last day of the feast of Tabernacles, Jesus exclaimed, "Let anyone who thirsts come to me and drink. Whoever believes in me, as scripture says:

'Rivers of living water will flow from within him.'"

John 7:37-38

This fifth word reveals the many thirsts of Jesus. On a physically human level, his body craves quenching relief. As one innocently condemned, he cries out for justice. In fulfilling his mission, he longs that we might partake of the waters and blood of salvation.

## LITANY

Placing the desires of Jesus in your heart, slowly pray this litany. The response to each petition is: "Jesus, help me to thirst."

For love and compassion ..................... Jesus, help me to thirst.
For peace and justice........................... Jesus, help me to thirst.
For understanding and respect........... Jesus, help me to thirst.
For your Body and Blood..................... Jesus, help me to thirst.
For your living waters........................... Jesus, help me to thirst.
For reconciliation among nations,
    families, and individuals.................. Jesus, help me to thirst.
For the Church and its mission........... Jesus, help me to thirst.
For those addicted to alcohol
    and drugs ........................................ Jesus, help me to thirst.
For those near death and those dying of cancer
    and AIDS.......................................... Jesus, help me to thirst.
For the elderly left abandoned ........... Jesus, help me to thirst.
For those who have no escape from
    the tyranny of poverty .................... Jesus, help me to thirst.
For jobs, health care, housing, decent education and the

distribution of food ........................... Jesus, help me to thirst.
For the unborn who will die ............... Jesus, help me to thirst.
For those who have disappeared, refugees, those living under
   repression and martial law ............... Jesus, help me to thirst.
For exploited workers and those persecuted because
   of their beliefs ................................... Jesus, help me to thirst.
For the depressed ................................. Jesus, help me to thirst.
For those who consume too much ... Jesus, help me to thirst.
For those who suffer due to promiscuity, infidelity,
   spouse and child abuse ................... Jesus, help me to thirst.
For those who diminish the human dignity of others
   because of their color, sex, creed, race, religion,
   or physical appearance .................... Jesus, help me to thirst.
For the physically impaired and the mentally
   and emotionally handicapped........ Jesus, help me to thirst.
For those who do not even know or care what it is to
   thirst..................................................... Jesus, help me to thirst.

## SUGGESTIONS FOR ACTION

   1) Reflect upon what you truly seek and desire? Be specific. How does the thirst of Jesus challenge these preferences and actions of your daily life, your work and leisure, your relationships?

   2) In praying the above litany, which petitions are the easiest to pray, which are the hardest? Realizing that Jesus thirsts for the entire human race, request from him the help to expand your thirsting, especially in those most difficult areas.

## PRAYER

As the deer longs for streams of water,
   so my soul longs for you, O God.

My being thirsts for God, the living God.
   When can I go and see the face of God?
My tears have been my food day and night,
   as they ask daily, "Where is your God?"
Those times I recall
   as I pour out my soul,
When I went in procession with the crowd,
   I went with them to the house of God,
Amid loud cries of thanksgiving,
   with the multitude keeping festival.
Why are you downcast, my soul;
   why do you groan within me?
Wait for God, whom I shall praise again,
   my savior and my God.

                              *Psalm 42:2-6*

# THE SIXTH WORD

## *The Prayer of Surrender*

*"Father, into your hands I commend my spirit."*
*Luke 23:46*

## SCRIPTURE

*It was now about noon and darkness came over the whole land until three in the afternoon because of an eclipse of the sun. Then the veil of the temple was torn down the middle. Jesus cried out in a loud voice, "Father, into your hands I commend my spirit"; and when he had said this he breathed his last. The centurion who witnessed what had happened glorified God and said, "This man was innocent beyond doubt." When all the people who had gathered for this spectacle saw what had happened, they returned home beating their breasts; but all his acquaintances stood at a distance, including the women who had followed him from Galilee and saw these events. Luke 23:44-49.*

## REFLECTION

Whatever might be our gauge of importance and success, the equalizing, impartial act of dying invites us to surrender our measurements of fame and achievement. Death quickly erases our misplaced illusions.

From the cross, what does Jesus teach us about approaching death? Jesus reviews his life, his dreams and hopes, the miracles and healings, the friendships, those who walked away, and those now present who want him dead more than anything else. He examines the journey to which he has been faithful. And, most importantly, during these last moments, Jesus continues to pray to the Father.

No one aspires for crucifixion. Jesus did not. The cross suggests no victory, no first place, no Olympic gold; it is the sign of failure. We cannot spiritualize or anesthetize Jesus' dying on the cross. We only do an injustice to what he experienced and diminish the force of the words he uttered.

With death quickly approaching, Jesus has very few actions left. Finally, Jesus commends himself to God. He places everything, especially the hidden mystery of death, in the greater mercy and care of the Father.

This sixth word, "Father, into your hands I commend my spirit," is Jesus' prayer of surrender. There is nothing more for Jesus to say or do except to hand over his journey and person into the compassionate hands of the Father. Jesus admits the failure of the cross and becomes powerless. There is no bargaining, no asking for a miracle, no polemic against injustice, or outburst of rage. Jesus lets go of what little remains: the pain, the thirst, the darkness, doubts, even his last breath. Jesus commits everything into the higher wisdom and understanding of the Father.

The prayer of surrender is a profound gesture of trust and confidence in God. To concede at any time is difficult, but to surrender from the humiliating injustice and failure of the cross only increases the significance of the letting go. From a powerless position, Jesus prays, "Father, into your hands—not according to my control, my will, my plans, but into your hands—I commend my spirit."

This prayer of surrender found in the sixth word is tied to three other essential prayer words from the cross: the fourth word, the fifth and the seventh. Together, these four words form a school of prayer.

The sixth word is the pivotal connection between the fourth and fifth words and the concluding seventh word. The prayer of surrender builds on the fourth word, "My God, my God, why have you forsaken me?" which is the prayer of the passions. The fifth word, "I thirst," further amplifies one's bodily and spiritual yearnings, and complements the content and emotional components necessary for the prayer of surrender.

Effective prayer needs to contain direct, unfiltered, human

experience, whether this might be our diverse thirstings or our raw feelings. Jesus, in the fourth and fifth words, models for us how to begin our prayer from the depths of our immediate experience—that is, where I am, how I am, stating clearly what I am experiencing and precisely how I am feeling.

Then, the sixth word becomes the second step in this three part prayer. Once we are in touch with our experience, Jesus invites us to surrender it, to hand it over to the Father. "Father, into your hands I commend my spirit." Lastly, the seventh word on the cross is the conclusion of the prayer of Jesus. This is the final amen, "It is finished."

## JESUS' SCHOOL OF PRAYER
Briefly, there are three important movements to the prayer of surrender:

1) Begin with the prayer of the passions, your lived experience coming forth from one's depths. The fourth and fifth word.

2) Next, the prayer of surrender, hand over to the Father this experience. The sixth word.

3) Lastly, truly finish the prayer with the amen of Jesus. The seventh word.

It is necessary to spend time with the prayer of surrender. This is a difficult prayer for us to learn because surrendering is foreign to us as a Western people. Our culture encourages us to control, to be powerful, to be in charge. In contrast, on the cross we find a countercultural Jesus who teaches us to pray as powerless, crucified, dominating no one, handing everything over to the Father.

Luke 23:46 can easily be adapted as a mantra to fit your

prayer needs. Use its structure as a base and just change the last word. The following are examples:

Father, into your hands I commend my person.
Father, into your hands I commend my life.
Father, into your hands I commend my journey.
Father, into your hands I commend my failure.
Father, into your hands I commend my disappointments.
Father, into your hands I commend my mediocrity.
Father, into your hands I commend my powerlessness.
Father, into your hands I commend my vulnerability.
Father, into your hands I commend my doubts.
Father, into your hands I commend my anger.
Father, into your hands I commend my hurt.
Father, into your hands I commend my mission.
Father, into your hands I commend my abandonment.
Father, into your hands I commend my brokenness.
Father, into your hands I commend my sorrow.
Father, into your hands I commend my desire not to be here.
Father, into your hands I commend my family.
Father, into your hands I commend my unfinished agenda.
Father, into your hands I commend this injustice.
Father, into your hands I commend this cross.

Jesus models for us to commit everything to the Father, the sorrowful and joyful mysteries of life, all that you are and have, to hand over the totality. Our ability to be powerless allows God to heal us on our journey and to embrace us as we truly are. The spirituality of surrendering to God requires a life-long process. Of course, certain days we are able to let go better than other days. However, if we postpone learning the prayer of surrender, we will face it unprepared at death. Perhaps we can learn how to surrender to the providential care of God in advance, through our daily abandonment to the Father?

## SUGGESTIONS FOR ACTION

To verbalize the prayer of surrender one does not have to spend long hours contemplating precisely what to hand over. A good clue is when you encounter an obstacle: that particular something, someone, circumstance, or some aspect of yourself you would like to change but cannot. Then, you are experiencing your minor Calvary.

1) Reflect over your past week. What were those experiences that you found difficult and especially tested you to the limit? What is your normal response in these circumstances? How can the prayer of surrender assist you to channel these encounters?

2) In relationship to yourself, your shadow side and secret self, how do you process these areas? What do you do with negative emotions, dominating fears and compulsions? These become rich areas to acknowledge and hand over to the Holy Spirit.

3) Is there a memory that saps your energy each time you recall it? Do you find yourself entertaining a certain event, conversation, or life experience that has become an emotional roadblock? Perhaps you have even sought help to deal with these experiences. Place these memories within the context of the prayer of surrender.

## PRAYER

Father, help me in my powerlessness.
Send the wisdom and strength of the Holy Spirit.
My deeper, truer self desires your healing
as I surrender these areas to you.

Father, into your hands I commend...
this day, this trial, this sorrow, this cross.
my resentment, prejudices, lack of generosity.
my helplessness, not knowing what to say or do.
my judging, worries, anger and hatred.
my family and how I would like them to be, even
though they are not.
my poor self-image, my lack of creativity and risk.
my blaming of others, my deceits and envy.
all the things I cannot tolerate and I detest.
my darkness, pettiness, jealousies.
my addictions, dysfunctional habits, and fixations.
my manipulations, perverseness, negativity.
my non-gospel, non-sacramental ways of living.

## SOUL OF CHRIST
Soul of Christ, sanctify me
Body of Christ, save me
Blood of Christ, inebriate me
Water from the side of Christ, wash me
Passion of Christ, strengthen me
O Good Jesus, hear me
Within your wounds hide me
Permit me not to be separated from thee
From the wicked one defend me
At the hour of my death call me
And bid me come to thee
That with thy saints I may praise thee
for ever and ever. Amen.

# THE SEVENTH WORD

# *The Final Amen*

*"It is finished." John 19:30*

## SCRIPTURE

*When Jesus had taken the wine, he said, "It is finished." And bowing his head, he handed over the spirit.*

*Now since it was preparation day, in order that the bodies might not remain on the cross on the sabbath, for the sabbath day of that week was a solemn one, the Jews asked Pilate that their legs be broken and they be taken down. So the soldiers came and broke the legs of the first and then of the other one who was crucified with Jesus. But when they came to Jesus and saw that he was already dead they did not break his legs, but one soldier thrust his lance into his side, and immediately blood and water flowed out. An eyewitness has testified, and his testimony is true; he knows that he is speaking the truth, so that you also may [come to] believe. John 19:30-35.*

## REFLECTION

The moment of death finally arrives. After enduring three hours on the cross, Jesus expresses the inevitable, "It is finished." Even still, a profound transition is taking place. Jesus spoke of this mystery in John 12:24: "Amen, amen, I say to you, unless a wheat grain falls into the ground and dies, it remains just a grain of wheat; but if it dies, it produces much fruit." This verse expresses the mystery of the Christian passage from life to death, from death to eternal life. Jesus did not divert the total emptying of his person and journey in God. Prior to bowing his head, he said for all generations to hear, "It is finished, it is accomplished, it is fulfilled." By Jesus' embracing death, life was changed, not ended.

At this pivotal moment of darkness, scripture became fulfilled and the mission of Jesus completed. Through the action of Jesus breathing his last, the glory of God fully took over his being. Death produces the greatest fruit of all, union with God.

In the seventeenth chapter of John, Jesus provides an insight into the significance of fulfilling the mission given to us by God. The entire chapter is referred to as the "Prayer of Jesus." Here Jesus speaks of the hour. This special "hour" has many levels of meaning. It is the gospel hour of scriptural completion, of finishing the work given to him, of reunion with the Father, the hour of emptying self, the hour of glory. In Hebrew, one of the meanings of glory is pregnant. The result of the emptying out of self is becoming glorified, or, becoming pregnant in God.

Ponder the depth of this prayer of Jesus. He prays to enter fully into union with the Father, and just as important, that we, his followers, may also participate in this glory.

## THE PRAYER OF JESUS

Father, the hour has come. Give glory to your son, so that your son may glorify you, just as you gave him authority over all people, so that he may give eternal life to all you gave him. Now this is eternal life, that they should know you, the only true God, and the one whom you sent, Jesus Christ. I glorified you on earth by accomplishing the work that you gave me to do. Now glorify me, Father, with you, with the glory that I had with you before the world began.

And everything of mine is yours and everything of yours is mine, and I have been glorified in them. And I will no longer be in the world, but they are in the world, while I am coming to you. Holy Father, keep them in your name that you have given me, so that they may be one just as we are." John 17:1-5,10-11.

Jesus is aware that nothing more remains to be said, nothing more to be done except that last of human acts, to die. There is no more blood left to be poured out, no more parables or beatitudes to convey. Everything is over and completed, the task finished, the gift of humanity's redemption and reconciliation accomplished. The death of Jesus reopens the pathway for all humanity to enter totally into God's presence and glory.

How can we apply this concluding statement of Jesus to our everyday experience? We can pray this seventh word in two ways: first, through daily discernment we can apply the final "Amen" of Jesus to those experiences that need to be embraced and to those that need to be completely finished and buried; second, we can make Jesus' last word our own concluding prayer at the hour of death.

First, the practice of daily discernment. As disciples of Jesus, the Father invites each of us in fidelity to complete the mission that is our privilege. The first way we can pray "It is fulfilled" is by staying true to our unique faith-journey. This discernment process entails a daily reflective awareness so that the gospel may become glorified in us.

Discernment also asks that we examine our behavior to insure that the gospel seed is planted in good soil. To discern is that adult process by which we consciously choose to cater no longer to those destructive actions and thoughts that need to be discarded. In this manner, the seventh word of Jesus is the critical conclusion to the prayer of surrender.

The art of discernment means that we creatively take authority over negative, non-gospel life patterns. To the kingdom of darkness, addictiveness, and selfishness, I say with Jesus, "It is finished." I do not have the luxury, the energy, or the time to engage in such activity or even to entertain such memories or illusions any longer. If the memory returns, address and inform it again with the words of Jesus, "It is finished." As disciples we are called to monitor the attitudes and spirits that we give access into our person.

There is a story of two monks who were returning to the monastery. At the riverbank they met an exceedingly beautiful woman. She wished to cross the river, but the water was too high and swift. Upon her request, the older monk lifted the woman on his back and carried her across. Upon arriving on the other side, they exchanged pleasantries and each party resumed the journey.

Now the younger monk was thoroughly scandalized. For two full hours he berated his companion on the flagrant violation of the holy rule: Had he forgotten that he was a monk? How dare he touch a woman, and actually carry her across the river? What would people say?

The older monk listened patiently to the interminable harangue. Finally, he interrupted, "My friend, I left the woman on the river's edge. Are you still carrying her?"

There are certain events in life that need to be left at the river's edge. The seventh word helps us say to those experiences, "It is over, finished, done," and then to go on with life.

The second way we can pray the seventh word is when we come face to face with the moment of our own death. In imitation of Jesus we can express from the heart, "Father, it is finished. I have done my best to accomplish the mission you gave me." Then, in the example of Jesus, bow your head and surrender your spirit.

## SUGGESTIONS FOR ACTION
Pray to the Holy Spirit for growth in two important virtues necessary for the journey: discerning wisdom and courage. Pray for wisdom to know your mission. Pray for courage to accomplish your mission, to fulfill it, to finish it.

1) Review this past week, or, if needed, a longer period of time. Is there some unfinished business or postponed reconciliation that needs to be addressed? Why not tackle

this issue today and bring it to completion? Pray to the Holy Spirit for the courage to finish those responsibilities that are yours to complete.

2) To remain constant in one's mission demands a discerning awareness. As you examine your lifestyle, what are those patterns, thoughts, or desires that are non-lifegiving and destructive? How do you deal with these tensions? As in the story of the two monks, is there anything that needs to be left at the riverbank? Pray to the Spirit for the discernment and creative authority to leave behind what needs to be finished once and for all.

3) Jesus entered into the glory of the Father through the complete emptying of self. So that the glory of the Father may produce a rich harvest, what do you need to let go of so that God's spirit may blossom?

## PRAYER

Glory be to the Father,
and to the Son,
and to the Holy Spirit.

As it was in the beginning,
is now,
and ever shall be,
world without end. Amen.

# EPILOGUE

# *Easter Pilgrimage*

*"Jesus himself drew near and walked with them."*
*Luke 24:15*

The following Easter passage from Luke contains twenty-two verses. Jesus walks with two downcast disciples. A gradual, unfolding relationship with the Jerusalem community is reestablished. The motif throughout this account is one of pilgrimage and faith development.

## SCRIPTURE

*Now that very day two of them were going to a village seven miles from Jerusalem called Emmaus, and they were conversing about all the things that had occurred. And it happened that while they were conversing and debating, Jesus himself drew near and walked with them, but their eyes were prevented from recognizing him. He asked them, "What are you discussing as you walk along?" They stopped, looking downcast. One of them, named Cleopas, said to him in reply, "Are you the only visitor to Jerusalem who does not know of the things that have taken place there in these days?" And he replied to them, "What sort of things?" They said to him, "The things that happened to Jesus the Nazarene, who was a prophet mighty in deed and word before God and all the people, how our chief priests and rulers both handed him over to a sentence of death and crucified him. But we were hoping that he would be the one to redeem Israel; and besides all this, it is now the third day since this took place. Some women from our group, however, have astounded us: they were at the tomb early in the morning and did not find his body; they came back and reported that they had indeed seen a vision of angels who announced that he was alive. Then some of those with us went to the tomb and found things just as the women had described, but him they did not see." And then he said to*

*them, "Oh, how foolish you are! How slow of heart to believe
all that the prophets spoke! Was it not necessary that the
Messiah should suffer these things and enter into his glory?"
Then beginning with Moses and all the prophets, he interpret-
ed to them what referred to him in all the scriptures. As they
approached the village to which they were going, he gave the
impression that he was going on farther. But they urged him,
"Stay with us, for it is nearly evening and the day is almost
over." So he went in to stay with them. And it happened that,
while he was with them at table, he took bread, said the blessing, broke it, and gave it to them. With that their eyes were
opened and they recognized him, but he vanished from their
sight. Then they said to each other, "Were not our hearts burning [within us] while he spoke to us on the way and opened
the scriptures to us?" So they set out at once and returned to
Jerusalem where they found gathered together the eleven and
those with them who were saying, "The Lord has truly been
raised and has appeared to Simon!" Then the two recounted
what had taken place on the way and how he was known to
them in the breaking of the bread. Luke 24:13-35*

## REFLECTION

In the various Easter accounts, the identity of the newly risen
Jesus is initially mistaken. In John 20:16, Mary Magdala
thought Jesus was a gardener. In John 21:4, Jesus is seen as
an ordinary person walking along the Galilee shore. In Luke
24:37, the disciples perceived Jesus as a ghost. They were
startled, terrified. Under what conditions, by what power, how
could anyone rise from the dead? Doubting Thomas refused
to believe the Apostles that they had truly seen the Lord. As a
condition of faith, Thomas demanded to place his hands into
the side of this allegedly risen Jesus.

While Jesus had spoken of his resurrection prior to his
death, the disciples did not fully comprehend its meaning.

They lacked the imagination and leap of faith to grasp the reality of Easter—so much so that in the presence of the risen Jesus they often did not recognize him. Perhaps we fail to recognize the diverse manifestations of Jesus as well: his presence in the Word, community, sacraments, the beauty of nature, or in the quiet resting of the Spirit in one's being.

At the Eucharist, following the consecration of the bread and wine, the assembly acclaims, "Christ has died, Christ is risen, Christ will come again." This concise formula is referred to as the mystery of faith. In credal fashion, it expresses the Christian transition from death to the rising of Easter, to the anticipation of Jesus coming again. While we pray and sing this acclamation which provides a clear faith focus, we need to keep in mind that the early Christians were grappling with the reality of Jesus' resurrection, his appearances, and his Easter words to them. Many times, they lacked the capacity to see and truly understand completely. They did not have the benefit of a faith maturation that has taken centuries to develop.

The account of the two disciples on the road to Emmaus offers many lessons for us as we face our own faith development challenges. Oftentimes, when we are so proximate to personal tragedy, loss, or crucifixion, we lose sight of the reassurance and meaning of the resurrection. We fumble as how to reinterpret our crises in the light of Easter.

Our perception becomes clouded like the Emmaus bound disciples who were dejected. There can be a tendency to walk away from the support of community. Here, the disciples discounted the story of the women who encountered the vision of angels at the tomb. This, in turn, affected what they were able to see and understand. They remained burnt out and depressed.

In the midst of such spiritual confusion, there is noted a divine compassion. Jesus is present as a fellow pilgrim, a companion on the way. However, the disciples, who are so caught up with their grief, literally do not recognize Jesus, his voice, or sociability of relating. Throughout this scene, Jesus demonstrates great patience in accepting the disciples where they were on their journey.  As Jesus teaches us from the cross how to pray, embrace life, and seek God, Jesus, as pilgrim, tolerantly assists us to reestablish our Easter faith once again.

## SUGGESTIONS FOR ACTION
What are some of the lessons that Luke 24 helps us remember when we experience our own dark nights? Luke reminds us that there are many ways to reconnect with Easter.

1) As you encounter distress, know that the compassionate Jesus walks as a friend with you on your journey.

2) In times of trial, notice if you have a tendency to walk away from the support of community toward separation and isolation. How can you take creative action to seek needed help?

3) Jesus empathetically listened to the disciples, their crisis and confusion. To whom do you pour out your doubts and grief? When people come to you, how does Jesus teach you to listen?

4) Jesus used the scriptures to come to a deeper understanding of suffering and glory. How do you learn from the Emmaus journey to use the wisdom of the Word as a means of comfort and guidance? What are your favorite passages that reconnect you with Jesus risen?

5) The disciples requested that the unrecognized Jesus stay and dine with them. They went out of their way to seek new company that was outgoing, healthy, and spiritual. What is the lesson here for you?

6) At table, Jesus took the bread, blessed it, broke it and gave it to the disciples. Along with an appreciation of the Word, the sacramental nourishment of the Eucharist is an essential component of living an Easter life. In times of distress, how do you partake of the wellspring of sacramental life?

7) Jesus spent an entire day on journey with the disciples. The images here are those of retreat and pilgrimage. In the midst of our confusion, Jesus spends quality time accepting us the way we are as we transition through stages of Easter healing. As you review the Emmaus story, what do you learn about your spiritual mending process?

8) The effect of Jesus' visit was that the hearts of the disciples were burning. With a renewed faith and insight, they returned to the Jerusalem community. In what ways do you nourish your heart so that it receives the attention it needs to live and love? The disciples underwent a conversion experience. What are the opportunities for conversion in your life? In your daily living, how can you better imitate the risen Jesus?

## PRAYER

Risen Jesus, Pilgrim and Friend,
as you did not turn away from Calvary,
   you stand by us as we experience our cross.
You are not far, but always near, by our side.
   You journey with us,
whether we face Jerusalem or not.
   You are the constant one
always inviting us to rediscover Easter and Pentecost.
   In the different seasons of our pilgrimage,
send your hovering Spirit of wisdom and courage

so that when we experience our valleys of darkness
we may be refreshed by the brightness of the resurrection.
  May we together, roll back the Good Friday burial stone,
and walk with one another as companions
  in the freedom of the radiance of Easter.

# NOTES

1) P. 15, edited story from *The Seven Last Words*, by Fulton J. Sheen, copyright 1993 by the Century Co., Alba House 1982 edition, p. 13.

2) P. 17, edited story from *Stories and Parables for Preachers and Teachers*, by Paul J. Wharton, copyright 1986, Paulist Press, p. 39.

3) P. 58, edited story from *Song of the Bird*, by Anthony de Mello, S.J., copyright 1982, Doubleday and Company, Inc., p. 138.